Make A Bundle Selling Bundles on Amazon!

By

Cordelia Blake

Publisher's Page

Copyright © 2018. Scanner Society & Cordelia Blake. All rights reserved.

No part of this book may be reproduced in any written, electronic, recording, or photocopy without the written permission of the publisher or author except in the case of brief quotations embedded in critical articles and reviews.

Although every precaution has been taken to verify the accuracy of the information contained herein, the author and publisher assume no responsibility for any errors or omissions. No liability is assumed for damages that may result from the use of information contained within.

First Printing: 2018

Introduction

This book is intended as a guide for people and companies already selling on Amazon. If you are new to the marketplace, consider an intro course or just go through every lesson at *Seller University* by Amazon (https://services.amazon.com/content/seller-resources-how-to-guides.html).

Amazon seller support does not care what I or any other "expert" told you to do when you get into trouble. So, please check everything with Amazon's terms of service (TOS) and engage in good business practices! While I do my best to give compliant instructions, no one is perfect, and the rules constantly change.

THANK YOU for reading this book. Please feel free to join our mailing list and learn more at (www.scannersociety.com) or email me at cordelia@scannersociety.com.

Chapter 1: What Is A Bundle?

A **BUNDLE**, on Amazon, is a group of different products that go together to make a better single product. The goal of a good bundle is for each product to compliment the others and to make the customer's life easier.

According to Seller Central, a bundle "provides convenience and value to buyers... bundles must consist of items that are highly complementary."

A Bundle Does...

Not include a primary product that is a video game, a book, or a DVD.

This bundle does NOT comply with Amazon Terms Of Service.

Include a book or DVD if it is secondary (for example, a yoga DVD and a yoga mat).

This bundle contains a book and is compliant with TOS.

From Amazon

A Bundle Listing Has…

- The word "Bundle" in the product title
- All the products in the bundle listed in the first bullet
- A main image with all the specific products in the bundle

> HINT: When researching, search for keywords and the word BUNDLE to see what other sellers are selling as bundles. All sellers are supposed to use the word BUNDLE in the title.

Bundles Can Be

Functional

- Simply combine a few products together such as a screwdriver and a hammer

Giftable

- A few items that together make a good gift.
- A bundle packaged for gifting could be simply a combo of products that together make a good present or could also include a gift bag.

Source VIA:

Arbitrage

This is good for seasonal or short-term bundles. It is also good for testing a small quantity of something that can be sourced via wholesale or private label in larger quantities later.

The Spotted Moose
The Spotted Moose Colorful Red and White 7 Piece Kitchen Linen Bundle With 2 Dish Towels, 2 Dish Cloths, 2 Potholders. and 1 Oven Mitt

★★★★★ ▾ 1 customer review

Price: **$16.99** & **FREE Shipping** on orders over $25 shipped by Amazon. Details
Get $10 off instantly! Pay $6.99 upon approval for the Amazon Prime Store Card.
✓prime | Try Fast, Free Shipping ▾
Only 15 left in stock - order soon.
Want it tomorrow, May 11? Order within 4 hrs 43 mins and choose **One-Day Shipping** at checkout. Details
Sold by The Spotted Moose and Fulfilled by Amazon. Gift-wrap available.

Color: **Red**

Wholesale

This is an excellent way to build scalable bundles. Combining products from different suppliers not only provides convenience to the customer but also is easy to re-order and becomes a replen. It is also difficult for others to replicate.

Private Label

Whether products are created from promotional products or imported, maximize their market appeal and cater to the customer by combining them.

A Blend!

Combining sourcing methods is a good way to protect a listing by keeping other sellers off of it. Custom ordering one or more complementary products to go with wholesale or arbitraged items makes it very hard for other sellers to share your listing. Just make sure that what you add is valuable to the customer and does not violate Amazon TOS.

Do Not Do This!

Adding a logo'd item that is unrelated to a bundle will neither help sales nor help the customer. In addition, it is a violation of TOS.

Combining products is always a good way to increase the average selling price (ASP) per SKU (stock keeping unit) and to have unique listings that are highly desirable to customers.

Chapter 2 - Bundle Building

How do I come up with ideas for bundles?

This is the biggest challenge in any retail environment. The major advantage that a smaller business has is that it can target smaller communities with products that they will love! This Chapter will cover SIX specific techniques for sourcing bundles.

1. Develop "Niche-Pertise"
2. Know An Avatar
3. Bad Listings With Good Rank
4. The Freebie
5. Don't Sell Someone A To-Do List

1. Develop Niche-Pertise

A niche is a specialized segment of the market for a particular kind of product or service. Understanding a community or type of customer and what it likes, wants, and has a perceived need for is the key to developing successful bundles.

Learn A Niche...

- From items that you've sold in the past
- From what you like
- From what your friends and family like
- From social media research

Niches are SPECIFIC by PRODUCT

Not Chocolate but...

White chocolate, dark chocolate, super dark chocolate, organic chocolate, fair trade chocolate, spicy chocolate, salty chocolate, chocolate with weird things in it (potato chips, crickets, ants, jalapeños)

Not Party Supplies but...

Retirement supplies, first birthday supplies, sweet sixteen supplies, quinceañera supplies, thirteenth supplies, supplies for girls, supplies for boys, gender neutral supplies, classy supplies, raunchy supplies, bridal shower supplies, high tea supplies, 80s party supplies, princess party supplies, ugly sweater party supplies

Not Father's Day but...

From kid, from adult kid, from "us", from mom, for grandpa, for dad, new dad, dads, from daughter, papa

A Few Examples

White Chocolate Easter Candy

Spicy Almond Snacks

2. Know An Avatar

What is an AVATAR?

Avatar is the marketing term used to describe a specific customer.

Avatars are SPECIFIC by CUSTOMER

Understand as many details about your customer as possible. **The most important things to know are customer PAIN POINTS and their fantasy self.** Solve their pain and help them live their fantasy and you'll sell products!

A Few Examples

People who LOVE

Their food: Organic, gluten free, keto, low carb, peanut free, retro

Their culture: Eritrean, Pakistani, Korean, Vietnamese, Italian, Thai, Filipino, Welsh, Chinese, Tibetan. Jewish…

Their vacation destination: Orlando, Hilton Head, Boston, San Francisco, Paris, Appalachian trail

People who have HOBBIES

Quilting, knitting, crocheting, sewing, doll clothes making, bowling, lacrosse, running, hiking, biking, zip lining, gaming

People who HAVE

Long hair, thick hair, curly hair, African-American hair, natural hair

Bundle Examples For Different Avatars

People who throw bridal showers and like flowers and games

Casual fishing hobbyists

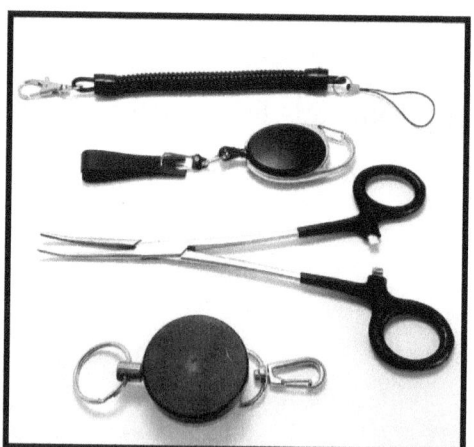

Indian food loving outdoor enthusiasts

How Do I Develop Niche-pertise and Know Avatars?

- Friends & family
- Products you've sold in the past
- Facebook Groups (join and learn)
- Blogs, Instagram & Pinterest
- Meetups
- Software tools
- Other products, improve on them

> TEST. If you strike a vein, keep on bundling; if not, move on and find a new one.

3. Bad Listings With Good Rank (BLGR)

Every listing on Amazon has a "rank," also called its Best Seller Rank or BSR. #1 is the BEST so the lower the BSR, the better the item is ranked in a category.

| Best Sellers Rank | #1 in Toys & Games (See Top 100 in Toys & Games) |

Or

| Best Sellers Rank | #2,757,518 in Home & Kitchen (See Top 100 in Home & Kitchen) |

> Recognizing bad listings with good rank (BLGR) is a good way to identify underserved niches.

PREMISE: Listing standards exist to help customers. If they buy something even when the listing is substandard, then they TRULY WANT IT.

BLGR = "TAKE MY MONEY"

What Makes A Listing Bad?

- **Images** are amateurish, unclear, not zoomable
- **Bullets** are not present, not clear, and don't specify what the customer will receive
- **Description** - what description?
- **Reviews** are poor or lacking

What Does A Bad Listing Tell You?

- **Product combos** - suggests things that customers want to buy together
- **Theme** - tells the type of product that is desired
- **BOLO Brands** - If it's so hot that the listing does not matter, look for similar products.

- **Niches** - BLGRs point to underserved niches and avatars

Example 1: Construction Party Supplies

This listing has a noncompliant image, and it's not totally clear what is included in it.

Example 2: Miniature Barbie Doll 12 Pack

Another noncompliant image: non-branded products are represented, the product title does not match the image, and MORE! However, parents do want their Barbie "style" party favors!

Use BLGR for INSPIRATION! Check out the keywords, the product combinations, and the concept, and use them to create your own successful bundles. Try to take the idea and improve on it.

4. Don't Sell Someone A To-Do List

For any product that you want to sell, think about the task that the customer will do with it, and then provide as many components to complete that task as possible.

Think about what your customers need, and try to include everything that they need in your bundle.

Look For Incomplete Things!

- In your niches
- In the **Bestsellers List**
    - https://www.amazon.com/Best-Sellers/zgbs
- In the **Movers & Shakers List**
    - https://www.amazon.com/gp/movers-and-shakers/ref=zg_bs_tab
- In your current popular inventory

| Best Sellers | New Releases | Movers & Shakers | Most Wished For | Gift Ideas |

Amazon Best Sellers
Our most popular products based on sales. Updated hourly.

Any Department
- Amazon Devices & Accessories
- Amazon Launchpad
- Appliances
- Apps & Games
- Arts, Crafts & Sewing
- Automotive
- Baby
- Beauty & Personal Care
- Books
- CDs & Vinyl
- Camera & Photo
- Cell Phones & Accessories
- Clothing, Shoes & Jewelry
- Collectible Coins
- Computers & Accessories
- Digital Music
- Electronics
- Entertainment Collectibles
- Gift Cards
- Grocery & Gourmet Food
- Health & Household
- Home & Kitchen
- Industrial & Scientific
- Kindle Store
- Kitchen & Dining
- Magazine Subscriptions
- Movies & TV
- Musical Instruments
- Office Products
- Patio, Lawn & Garden
- Pet Supplies

Toys & Games
- See more Best Sellers in Toys & Games

1.
Dynasty Toys Laser Tag Set and Carrying Case for Kids Multiplayer 4 Pack
★★★★★ 843

2.
DYNASTY TOYS Girls Toys Pink Laser Tag Blaster and Flipping Robot Bug/Spider Target - Perfect Night Time...
★★★★★ 72

3.
L.O.L. Surprise! Surprise Confetti Pop- Series 3 Collectible Dolls
★★★★★ 54

Electronics
- See more Best Sellers in Electronics

1.
Fire TV Stick with Alexa Voice Remote | Streaming Media Player
★★★★★ 170,273

2.
Echo Dot (2nd Generation) - Smart speaker with Alexa - Black
★★★★★ 110,286

3.
Echo (2nd Generation) - Smart speaker with Alexa - Charcoal Fabric
★★★★★ 24,629

| Best Sellers | New Releases | Movers & Shakers | Most Wished For | Gift Ideas |

Amazon Movers & Shakers
Our biggest gainers in sales rank over the past 24 hours. Updated hourly.

Any Department
- Amazon Devices & Accessories
- Amazon Launchpad
- Appliances
- Apps & Games
- Arts, Crafts & Sewing
- Automotive
- Baby
- Beauty & Personal Care
- Books
- CDs & Vinyl
- Camera & Photo
- Cell Phones & Accessories
- Clothing, Shoes & Jewelry
- Collectible Coins
- Computers & Accessories
- Digital Music
- Electronics
- Entertainment Collectibles
- Gift Cards
- Grocery & Gourmet Food
- Health & Household
- Home & Kitchen
- Kindle Store
- Kitchen & Dining
- Magazine Subscriptions
- Movies & TV
- Musical Instruments
- Office Products
- Patio, Lawn & Garden
- Pet Supplies
- Phone, Pantry
- Software
- Sports & Outdoors
- Sports Collectibles

Books
- See more Movers & Shakers in Books

1. ↑ 476,727%
Sales rank: 19 (was 90,856)
Just Jessie: My Guide to Love, Life, Family, and Food
Jessie James Decker

2. ↑ 27,059%
Sales rank: 18 (was 4,384)
The Hundred-Year Marathon: China's Secret Strategy to Replace America as the Global...
Michael Pillsbury
★★★★★ 177

3. ↑ 1,285%
Sales rank: 60 (was 1,275)
The Conscious Parent: Transforming Ourselves, Empowering Our Children
- Dr Shefali Tsabary
★★★★★ 627

Camera & Photo
- See more Movers & Shakers in Camera & Photo

1. ↑
Sales rank: 20 (previously unranked)

Zmodo Wireless Security Camera System (4 pack) Smart HD Outdoor WiFi IP Cameras with Night Vision
★★★★☆ & 165

2. ↑
Sales rank: 75 (previously unranked)
 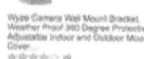
Wyze Camera Wall Mount Bracket, Weather Proof 360 Degree Protective Adjustable Indoor and Outdoor Mount Cover...
★★★★★ 29

3. ↑
Sales rank: 348 (previously unranked)

Canon EOS Rebel 7B DSLR Camera with 18-55mm and 75-300mm Lenses and Bag + 64GB Memory Card and Software Bundle

Drill down into subcategories for more inspiration and ideas. A good find is:

- A product that you can source
- A product that you are allowed to sell
- An additional something(s) that you identify that will enhance the customer experience
- Something that you are able to source too!

Example 1: Auto caddy

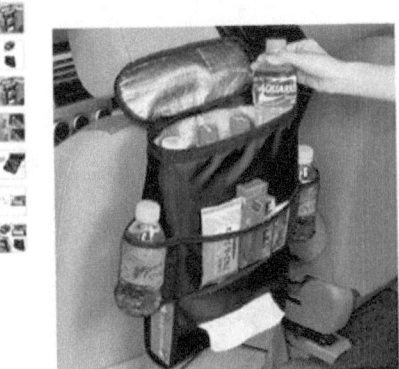 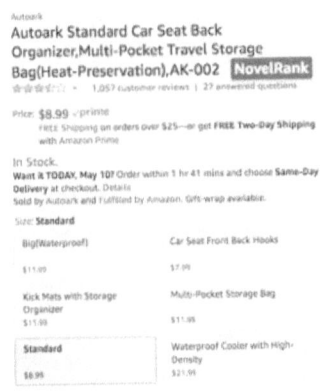

This was in the top 40 products in Automotive at the time of publication. Here are some products that could be bundled with this caddy from Dollar Tree to make the customer's experience even better.

Sesame Street Fragrance-Free Hushables Baby Wipes, 72-ct. Packs

Assured Antibacterial Bandages, 40-ct. Boxes

Carepak Travel-Size Essential First Aid Kits, 21 pc.

Example 2: Egg Cooker

The egg cooker above was in the top 100 Movers & Shakers in Kitchen at the time of publication. The hard-boiled egg slicer shown below could be bundled with the egg cooker (assuming that you could source it at the right price and that it is readily available either wholesale or even from a promotional supply company so that it could be customized).

5. The Freebie

Create a bundle by including a very low cost item with a single product that both adds value and can be included for essentially the same cost. Do not use the word FREE in the TITLE of the listing. Just include it, and price your bundle the same as the main product alone so that the customers are enticed to buy the bundle rather than the single item.

Example 1: The Spiralizer

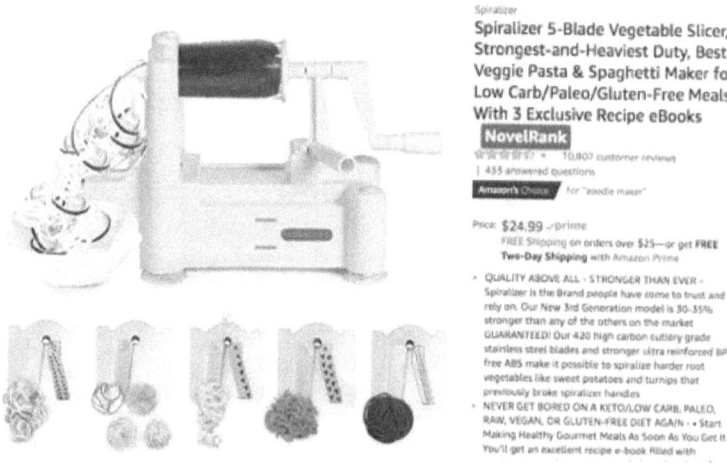

This is a popular product. Assuming that you could source it for a good ROI (return on investment), you could add a Dollar Store cleaning brush to it as a bundle. Those little sharp metal cutters are hard to clean!

Example 2: Colored Pencils

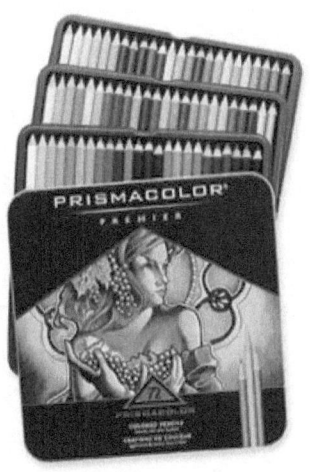 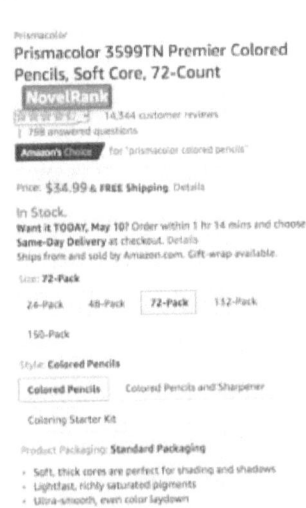

These are high-end art coloring pencils. Once again, assuming that they could be sourced at a good price, a nice handheld pencil sharpener could be added to make it a bundle. These are available at office supply stores and even

www.ScannerSociety.com

from promotional products companies, and they can be customized with a phrase or image that the customer would like.

6. Brand Recognition

Put popular brands or brands that customers like with non-branded products that complement them. Keep in mind that Amazon TOS specifically states that misrepresenting your bundle components as all coming from the "big" brand when they do not is against policy. You can combine products from multiple vendors who carry similar brands or licenses, for example, six Batman items from three different vendors.

Since people are very brand loyal, you can make customers happy by combining products for which they are looking!

Of course, there are some gray areas. Would combining black plates with Batman napkins be confusing to the customer? Like everything else that we do, all sellers have to make their own decisions.

Example 1: Batman Party Supplies

LEGO
Lego Batman Movie Deluxe Party Balloon Decorating Bundle
★★★★☆ ▾   3 customer reviews

Price: **$17.95** ✓prime
FREE Shipping on orders over $25—or get FREE Two-Day Shipping with Amazon Prime

In Stock.
Want it tomorrow, Sept. 23? Order within 3 hrs 26 mins and choose Saturday Delivery at checkout. Details
Sold by RAPID-N-GUARANTEED and Fulfilled by Amazon. Gift-wrap available.

- 1 Huge Lego Batman 23 Inch Mylar Balloon
- 1 Huge Batman Emblem 27 Inch Mylar Balloon

This bundle is a mix of licensed and black and yellow products. The seller does a good job of capturing brand loyal fans and providing value to the customer without misrepresenting the non-branded products .

Example 2: Minion Camp Set

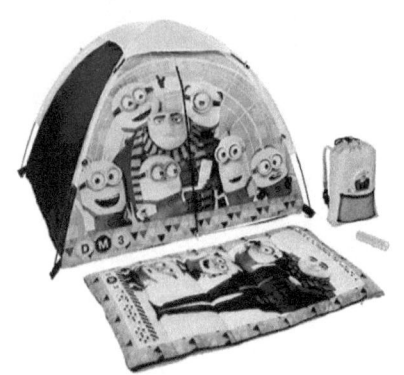

Here is another branded bundle with a mix of products from different suppliers.

Take ACTION!

- ❏ Practice spotting hot opportunities using each strategy.
    1. **Developing "Niche-Pertise"**
    2. **Knowing An Avatar**
    3. **Bad Listings With Good Rank (BLGR)**
    4. **Don't Sell Someone A To-Do List**
    5. **The Freebie**
    6. **Brand Recognition**
- ❏ Buddy up with a friend or two. Call it a mastermind, brainstorming, or accountability group and do it!
- ❏ IMPLEMENT. Try selling 3-6 units of a new bundle to test it. Learn from each one. Launch 2-10 bundles a month.

Chapter 3: The Process

Arbitrage Bundles

Using Retail or Online Arbitrage to build a bundle can be a good way to test a niche or avatar and build the confidence to order on a larger scale. Some bundles can be sourced long-term via arbitrage, but with Amazon cracking down on brands and other factors, it's important to be cautious and not go too deep.

Start with 3 – 6 units for each bundle, then progressively do more for the same target customer.

- Some sites to try:
    - Dollar Tree (open a wholesale account)
    - Oriental Trading
    - Walmart (apply for tax exempt status)

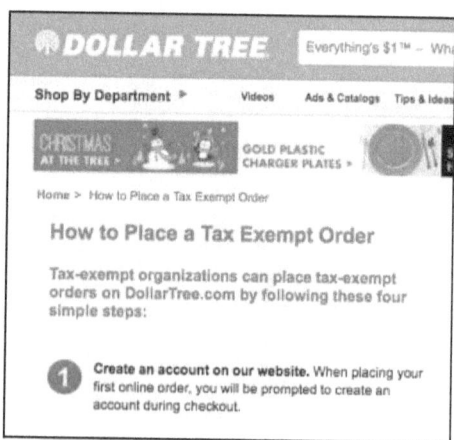

Wholesale Bundles

Looking for suppliers for bundle components is easier than finding overall profitable products to sell on Amazon. Just make sure that if the product is licensed (e.g., Batman), the company is legitimate and has the rights to use the license. Do not order licensed or branded merchandise from liquidation companies or international suppliers such as Aliexpress or Alibaba.

Represent yourself professionally, but do not lie about your company. If you are a smaller operation that's ok. It is better to find brands who are willing to work with you than to lie or misrepresent yourself. However, you should have a brochure style website and a professional email. Be your best self, but still be yourself!

Be prepared to CALL. Have a generic voicemail on your phone in case suppliers call back. Many sellers wonder if wholesalers will sell to Amazon sellers. Bundles can be your way in. Here is an example of an initial contact letter:

> Dear …,
>
> We sell gift baskets online and would like to use some of your products in an upcoming basket. We love their quality and value. How can we set up an account?
>
> Thank you,

Even if you are not actually selling a gift basket per se, you can use this phrasing. Most companies do not know the term "bundle." Alternatively, you could call them activity sets, kits, or whatever. Just use a word that makes sense to the company.

Suppliers may ask questions about your process and what you sell. Make it clear that you are creating your own products and not competing on their current listings. In addition, offer to share your store information with them, if needed, and always be willing to enforce MAP (their requested) pricing.

When using Google and Trade show sites (ASD Online, America's Mart, etc.) to find suppliers, it's easier if you search for specific items rather than general suppliers. For example, finding "organic tea in cloth bags wholesale" is easier on Google than finding "wholesale tea.".

Consider sourcing retail and paying full price to test your bundle before diving into a larger wholesale order. Many wholesalers will sell a smaller quantity if you pay for shipping. While your first batch of bundles may not be profitable, you will learn valuable information, and then, if the bundle is successful, you can order in a larger quantity.

When packaging your bundle, consider that it will be knocked around in a warehouse and in the shipping process, so protect it accordingly.

If you are planning to build a brand (see our *Brand Registry* section later in this book), you may want to order branded stickers to customize your packaging initially. Even though stickers are not compliant with Amazon's brand registry packaging guidelines, it will help to establish the name in the mind of the customer.

Packaging, like everything else, can evolve over time, so start with the simplest type, such as a plain cardboard box or polybag and go from there. Some good sources of supplies are:

- Bubblefast.com (The owners of Bubblefast are also Amazon sellers, so they know exactly what we need!)
- PaperMart
- Amazon
- Uline

Always check your bundle for both current and future profitability. It may be lower margin when you start at a lower volume, but make sure that at a reasonable velocity it has a good ROI (return on investment). When you look at your profit level, consider the amount of time that it takes to prep the bundle. Your time is an investment too! Think long and hard about the cost that you can realistically charge, and make sure that it still makes sense. While some bundles will sell for higher than you expect, others will sell for lower, so it's important to make sure that there is a healthy margin.

Finding Suppliers From Your Tribe

While many sellers may not want to share their specific best-selling products, they are often willing to share supplier names. Ask them!

In addition, ask every wholesaler with whom you communicate if it has a referral for you. "Do you know of a company that sells _____?" or "I am looking for a supplier of _____; do you have any ideas?"

Non-Amazon folks can be good sources too. People have many jobs that interact with wholesalers, so your "regular" friends may have contacts as well.

Private Label (Manufacturing)

Historically, what is now called "Private Label" by many was actually just manufacturing. Basically, it now means sourcing your own products and putting your own "mark" on them. Some are just replicas of other products, while others are different or unique in some way.

Private label bundling can be done in a few different ways. You can have one element made, such as a cup or chip clip that complements your other products and that also makes it harder for that bundle to be copied. Promotional product companies are a good place to source these items. **Keep in mind when ordering these products that they can be imprinted with a unique saying or word cloud, and it does not have to be just a logo.**

Another way to private label is to have a product manufacturer label a current product with your own label and brand. This can be done in large quantities from US-based manufacturers for everything from meat claws to pop sockets to tea to snack mix! They are still the legal manufacturer, but you are the brand owner of the branded product.

Alternatively, if you have your own products manufactured in China, the US, or somewhere else, don't just list them solo, but list them as bundles and multipacks!

> PUBLIC SERVICE ANNOUNCEMENT: Please use actual stuff that customers WANT and that make the bundle better! No free e-books with useless information or highlighter pens.

CreateSpace can be your friend. Learn how to create actual books and add those to relevant bundles. Types of books that can be created with some assistance from stock image companies and helpers are:

- Cookbooks
- Coloring books
- Journals
- Workbooks
- Inspirational books
- Diaries
- Notebooks

Costs to receive copies of a book that you create are usually less than $3 each. If you can create one that is a good quality product, it will enhance your bundle and make it competitor proof!

Chapter 4: Listing Basics

There are many books and courses about listings alone. We have a course, and there are other good ones out there too. Larger companies even have entire teams whose full time jobs are just to tweak listings! So, while writing a good listing can seem daunting, like everything else, **dig in and do your best, and you will improve over time**. Here are a few guidelines to start you off:

- Images
    - Primary image should be at least 1001 pixels square so that it is zoomable (1001 x 1001px)
    - Use the Amazon Seller app to take pictures or just use a good phone
    - Investing in a photo set-up over time may make sense, but you can start on a nice day outside with poster board from the dollar store as a backdrop
    - Use manufacturer pictures as often as possible, and compose them in graphics software rather than in "real life." A nicer and clearer digital image is usually better than the results from an amateur photographer
    - Make sure that main images are on a pure white background (best achieved with graphics software - try

www.clippingmagic.com) or use a service like www.pixelz.com
- Key words
    - Develop as comprehensive a list as you can. Use Amazon, Google, and simply looking at similar listings to start yourself off. Auto fill is a useful trick to find words! Once you have your "hotlist" of words, use them in the title, bullets, keywords, and description of your listing.
    - Try to keep your words relevant. Think about words that describe not only what your product IS but also who uses it and for what occasions or purposes it can be used.
    - There is no bonus for using the same word a million times. Once is enough.
    - Amazon extrapolates singulars and plurals, so if you have the word PEOPLE in your listing, there is no need to put PERSON too.
    - Amazon does not extrapolate related words, for example, teen and teenager, camp and camper and camping. Include all related forms.
- Write it so that PEOPLE will like it
    - Include its benefits and features. It's not just 2 inches tall, but it is portable, fits in a purse or pocket, and is always there when you need it!
    - Pre-answer likely customer questions. You can find out what customers want to know

by talking to them (it's old fashioned, but it works), by looking at reviews/complaints on similar listings, and by searching online.
- You will need either a UPC or GTIN Exemption when listing your bundle

Shameless Self Plug - Our class, **Amazon Listings Demystified** is an amazing course about how to write listings that both humans and algorithms will love. Once you have your listing squared away, you'll be ready for Pay Per Click.

INFO: www.ScannerSociety.com/listings
Use Code BUNDLEBOOK50 for $50 off

Scanner Society Members Receive A Much Larger Discount.

ACK! What If…Someone STEALS my listing???

Technically, the listing belongs to Amazon, but if someone else comes on, don't panic. Just keep on building more valuable bundles over time, and use some of our techniques to protect them. Some tips to protect your bundles are:

- Source from several vendors
- Include unique or hard-to-find products
- Find and have a better price

Do test buys of the other product. That bundle may not have all the right things in it. If it does not, then you can report it to Amazon.

UPC Codes

These barcodes/number combos are unique to each product.

The overseeing body for official and legitimate barcodes is the GS1.

- www.Gs1US.org
- They cost for the first year:
    - 10 for $250 ($25 each), 100 for $750 ($7.50 each), 1000 for $2500 ($2.50 each)
- Each additional year:
    - 10 for $50, 100 for $150, 1000 for $500
- Each product is registered individually by its barcode at the GS1

What about buying codes on eBay?

- This is against Amazon TOS because they are sometimes validating the brand and code on the GS1 database. Many people still do it, but it's a risky practice
- Any barcode that is not officially registered to your business and your brand or the business or brand of the manufacturer is not legitimate, no matter what their website says.
    - Know the risks!
        - You can simply be notified that you can't sell the item any longer
        - The listing can be shut down
        - Your account could be suspended

GTIN Exemption

This is an exemption by Amazon by category or brand. GTIN stands for Global Trade Item Number. You can apply for an exemption, and then individual products can be assigned an ASIN (Amazon Standard Identification Number) without a UPC or GTIN.

- For instructions, search for "How to list products that do not have a GTIN (UPC, EAN, JAN, or ISBN)" on Seller Support

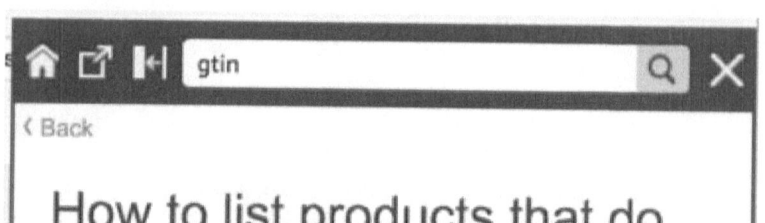

Request a GTIN Exemption from Amazon

"We require below mentioned information and documents to request for a GTIN Exemption. Review the list and get them ready before submitting the request:"

- **"Support letter from brand owner**, manufacturer or publisher to prove that they do not provide a GTIN for the products, or a **list of sample products for review**.
- We need a **website link to view the products**. If you do not have a website, nor does the brand or publisher have it, **you can upload pictures to an online image service** and provide us with the link.
- Support letter from brand owner, manufacturer or publisher"

Instructions for GTIN Exemption:
https://sellercentral.amazon.com/gp/help/200426310

Request An Exemption Here:
https://sellercentral.amazon.com/gtinx

In The Case Of Most Bundles, YOU ARE THE BRAND OWNER

Suspension Prevention & Brand Registry

You can create a brand of bundles similar to any other brand and register it on Amazon. You can work your way up to this. As you build your business...

- Obtain permission in writing from wholesalers to sell online in gift baskets if you are scaling
- Only use the brand name in your title if you have permission and if all the products in the bundle are from that brand. You can use it in the bullets if it's in a component
- As you scale, consider branded packaging
- More info on Suspension Prevention and Bundles? Go to the PRO, **Cynthia Stine** of *EGrowth Partners*:
    - https://egrowthpartners.com/blog/More-Amazon-Bundles-of-Joy
    - https://www.egrowthpartners.com/blog/bundles-opt-outs

Bundle Hack #1

Check "Add A Product" for out of stock bundles. You can jump on the listing or use it as a launching point for a new bundle

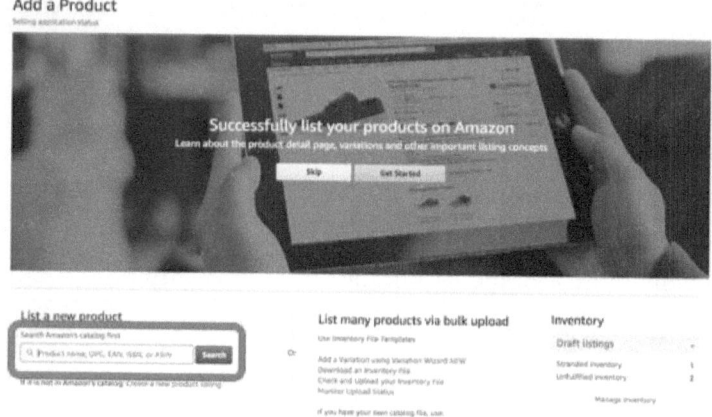

Bundle Hack #2

The company OrientalTrading.com has a great holiday calendar. It also can be a good source of bundle components for holidays.

Test and Restock

Start out with a quantity of 6-10 units. With each new bundle or holiday, incrementally increase the number of units as you learn to scale responsibly.

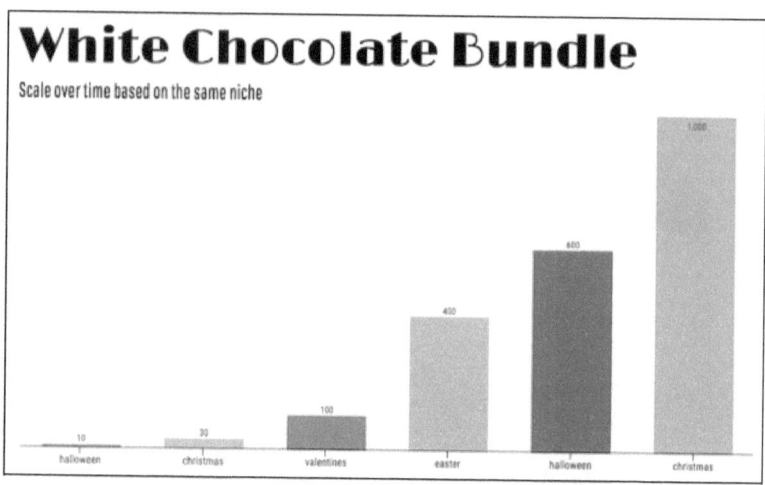

Off Amazon Bundles

On Amazon and other marketplace sites, we are creating bundles for our customers. One of the benefits of building an off-Amazon website is that you can actually let customers build their own bundles from the products that you sell!

Join our mailing list to stay up to date about Amazon selling and e-commerce news and updates.
www.ScannerSociety.com/UpdateMe

Join our community to be a part of the best group of Amazon Sellers around! Use this code: BUNDLEBOOK19 or follow this link to join for just $19.99 a month (normally $39).
www.ScannerSociety.com/BundleBook

Some Of The Benefits:

- Free & Discounted Training
- Private FB Group With Like Minded Sellers
- Members Only Podcast & Show
- Discounts On Events, Services, Classes, & Software
- Be Part Of A Long Term Membership Community That's Been Around Since 2013 With Many Members Who Have STAYED!

You will receive a FREE copy of this book as an e-book and the course as well.

Take the ONLINE COURSE,
Make A Bundle Selling Bundles On Amazon for just $9.99 on UDEMY.
https://www.ScannerSociety.com/BundleCourse9.99

TAKE ACTION! Bundle, Sell, & Repeat!

Resources:

Bundle Strategies

1. Develop "Niche-Pertise"
2. Know An Avatar
3. Bad Listings With Good Rank (BLGR)
4. Don't Sell Someone A To-Do List
5. The Freebie
6. Brand Recognition

Action Helpers!
- 10 Pages of Brainstorming Worksheets
- 10 Weeks of Weekly Planners

Brainstorm Pages!

Product: _____

What Does The Customer Do With It?

1. _____
2. _____
3. _____

What Else Could Be Bundled With It?

1. _____
2. _____
3. _____

How Can I Improve It?

1. _____
2. _____
3. _____

Other Ideas?

1. _____
2. _____
3. _____

Notes

_____

_____

Product: _____

What Does The Customer Do With It?

4. _____
5. _____
6. _____

What Else Could Be Bundled With It?

4. _____
5. _____
6. _____

How Can I Improve It?

4. _____
5. _____
6. _____

Other Ideas?

4. _____
5. _____
6. _____

Notes

_____

_____

Product: _____

What Does The Customer Do With It?

7. _____
8. _____
9. _____

What Else Could Be Bundled With It?

7. _____
8. _____
9. _____

How Can I Improve It?

7. _____
8. _____
9. _____

Other Ideas?

7. _____
8. _____
9. _____

Notes

_____

_____

Product:

_____

What Does The Customer Do With It?

10. _____
11. _____
12. _____

What Else Could Be Bundled With It?

10. _____
11. _____
12. _____

How Can I Improve It?

10. _____
11. _____
12. _____

Other Ideas?

10. _____
11. _____
12. _____

Notes

_____

_____

Product:
_____

What Does The Customer Do With It?

    13. _____

    14. _____

    15. _____

What Else Could Be Bundled With It?

    13. _____

    14. _____

    15. _____

How Can I Improve It?

    13. _____

    14. _____

    15. _____

Other Ideas?

    13. _____

    14. _____

    15. _____

Notes

_____

_____

Product:

_____

What Does The Customer Do With It?

16. _____
17. _____
18. _____

What Else Could Be Bundled With It?

16. _____
17. _____
18. _____

How Can I Improve It?

16. _____
17. _____
18. _____

Other Ideas?

16. _____
17. _____
18. _____

Notes

_____

_____

Brainstorm Pages!

Product:

_____

What Does The Customer Do With It?

19. _____

20. _____

21. _____

What Else Could Be Bundled With It?

19. _____

20. _____

21. _____

How Can I Improve It?

19. _____

20. _____

21. _____

Other Ideas?

19. _____

20. _____

21. _____

Notes

_____

_____

Brainstorm Pages!

Product:

_____

What Does The Customer Do With It?

22. _____

23. _____

24. _____

What Else Could Be Bundled With It?

22. _____

23. _____

24. _____

How Can I Improve It?

22. _____

23. _____

24. _____

Other Ideas?

22. _____

23. _____

24. _____

Notes

_____

_____

Brainstorm Pages!

Product:

_____

What Does The Customer Do With It?

    25. _____
    26. _____
    27. _____

What Else Could Be Bundled With It?

    25. _____
    26. _____
    27. _____

How Can I Improve It?

    25. _____
    26. _____
    27. _____

Other Ideas?

    25. _____
    26. _____
    27. _____

Notes

_____

_____

Brainstorm Pages!

Product:

_____

What Does The Customer Do With It?

28. _____
29. _____
30. _____

What Else Could Be Bundled With It?

28. _____
29. _____
30. _____

How Can I Improve It?

28. _____
29. _____
30. _____

Other Ideas?

28. _____
29. _____
30. _____

Notes

_____

_____

Brainstorm Pages!

Product:

_____

What Does The Customer Do With It?

31. _____
32. _____
33. _____

What Else Could Be Bundled With It?

31. _____
32. _____
33. _____

How Can I Improve It?

31. _____
32. _____
33. _____

Other Ideas?

31. _____
32. _____
33. _____

Notes

_____

_____

Weekly Action Plans

Start Day:

Day 1: Goals

1. _____
2. _____
3. _____
4. _____
5. _____

Notes

_____
_____
_____
_____
_____

Day 7: Accomplishments

1. _____
2. _____
3. _____
4. _____
5. _____

www.ScannerSociety.com

Weekly Action Plans

Start Day:

Day 1: Goals

6. _____
7. _____
8. _____
9. _____
10. _____

Notes

_____
_____
_____
_____
_____

Day 7: Accomplishments

6. _____
7. _____
8. _____
9. _____
10. _____

www.ScannerSociety.com

Weekly Action Plans

Start Day:

Day 1: Goals

11. _____
12. _____
13. _____
14. _____
15. _____

Notes

_____
_____
_____
_____
_____

Day 7: Accomplishments

11. _____
12. _____
13. _____
14. _____
15. _____

www.ScannerSociety.com

Weekly Action Plans

Start Day:

Day 1: Goals

16. _____
17. _____
18. _____
19. _____
20. _____

Notes

_____
_____
_____
_____
_____

Day 7: Accomplishments

16. _____
17. _____
18. _____
19. _____
20. _____

Weekly Action Plans

Start Day:

Day 1: Goals

21. _____
22. _____
23. _____
24. _____
25. _____

Notes

_____
_____
_____
_____
_____

Day 7: Accomplishments

21. _____
22. _____
23. _____
24. _____
25. _____

Weekly Action Plans

Start Day:

Day 1: Goals

26. _____
27. _____
28. _____
29. _____
30. _____

Notes

_____
_____
_____
_____
_____

Day 7: Accomplishments

26. _____
27. _____
28. _____
29. _____
30. _____

Weekly Action Plans

Start Day:

Day 1: Goals

31. _____
32. _____
33. _____
34. _____
35. _____

Notes

_____
_____
_____
_____
_____

Day 7: Accomplishments

31. _____
32. _____
33. _____
34. _____
35. _____

Weekly Action Plans

Start Day:

Day 1: Goals

36. _____
37. _____
38. _____
39. _____
40. _____

Notes

_____
_____
_____
_____
_____

Day 7: Accomplishments

36. _____
37. _____
38. _____
39. _____
40. _____

Weekly Action Plans

Start Day:

Day 1: Goals

41. _____
42. _____
43. _____
44. _____
45. _____

Notes

_____
_____
_____
_____
_____

Day 7: Accomplishments

41. _____
42. _____
43. _____
44. _____
45. _____

Weekly Action Plans

Start Day:

Day 1: Goals

46. _____
47. _____
48. _____
49. _____
50. _____

Notes

_____
_____
_____
_____
_____

Day 7: Accomplishments

46. _____
47. _____
48. _____
49. _____
50. _____

www.ScannerSociety.com

Notes:

Join our mailing list to stay up to date about Amazon selling and e-commerce news and updates.
www.ScannerSociety.com/UpdateMe

Join our community to be a part of the best group of Amazon Sellers around! Use this code: BUNDLEBOOK19 or follow this link to join for just $19.99 a month (normally $39).
www.ScannerSociety.com/BundleBook

Some Of The Benefits:

- Free & Discounted Training
- Private FB Group With Like Minded Sellers
- Members Only Podcast & Show
- Discounts On Events, Services, Classes, & Software
- Be Part Of A Long Term Membership Community That's Been Around Since 2013 With Many Members Who Have STAYED!

You will receive a FREE copy of this book as an e-book and the course as well.

Take the ONLINE COURSE, *Make A Bundle Selling Bundles On Amazon* for just $9.99 on UDEMY.
https://www.ScannerSociety.com/BundleCourse9.99

TAKE ACTION! Bundle, Sell, & Repeat!

www.ingramcontent.com/pod-product-compliance
Lightning Source LLC
Chambersburg PA
CBHW031539210526
45464CB00003B/1075